# WORKING IN

# SPORTS AND RECREATION

exploring
careers

# WORKING IN

# SPORTS AND RECREATION

### By Barbara Lee
### Introduction by Barbara Sher

Lerner Publications Company • Minneapolis

*For Ben, Molly, and Timothy*

*Acknowledgments*
My thanks to the dozen people profiled in
this book, who freely gave me hours of their
time. And thanks also to the many friends
and strangers—too many to name here—
who helped me find just the right people
to interview.

The Exploring Careers series was developed
by Barbara Lee

Copyright © 1996 by Barbara Lee

Library of Congress Cataloging-in-Publication Data

Lee, Barbara, 1945–
      Working in sports and recreation / Barbara Lee.
         p.   cm. — (Exploring Careers)
      Includes index.
      Summary: A behind-the-scenes tour of a dozen ways to earn a
   living in the world of sports and recreation, including practical
   tips to help explore such a career.
      ISBN 0-8225-1762-0 (alk. paper)
      1. Sports—Vocational guidance—United States—Juvenile
   literature. 2. Recreation—Vocational guidance—United States—
   Juvenile literature. [1. Sports—Vocational guidance. 2.
   Recreation—Vocational guidance. 3. Vocational guidance.]
   I. Title. II. Series:
      Exploring careers (Minneapolis, Minn.)
   GV734.L44  1996
   796'.023—dc20                                        95-46030

Manufactured in the United States of America
1  2  3  4  5  6  –  JR  –  01  00  99  98  97  96

# CONTENTS

# INTRODUCTION

## by Barbara Sher

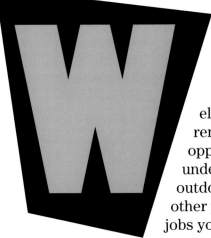

elcome to the world of work. It's a remarkable world, filled with opportunities, almost too big to understand. There are indoor jobs and outdoor jobs. There are jobs that involve other people and jobs that don't. There are jobs you've never heard of and jobs with names you can't pronounce. And to complicate matters even more, the jobs of tomorrow may not be the same as the jobs of today.

But some things will remain the same. In fact, let me tell you a secret. For successful people, work is like play. That's right—play. That's because they've found the work that is best suited to who they are. Their careers fit their unique talents, their interests, and their skills and education.

Begin by asking yourself what you love doing. What is fun? What makes you excited? The answers will give you some clues about what kind of work you might enjoy—and be good at. It's not too early to begin exploring. Talk to your teachers and parents, your friends and neighbors. Ask them to introduce you to people doing work that you would like to find out more about. You will be surprised by how willing people are to talk about what they do. Perhaps they will even show you around their workplaces.

Reading this book is a great start. Without leaving your chair, you will go to work with people who will tell you about what they do and why they do it. They will give you ideas. Maybe their jobs will seem boring or hard. Or maybe they'll excite you. It doesn't matter. It's all part of exploring.

So let yourself be curious. Be a detective. Remember, you don't have to make up your mind right now. You are just collecting information. Good luck. And have fun!

# TWELVE CAREERS IN SPORTS AND RECREATION

From professional sports heroes to dedicated Olympians chasing gold in faraway places to lone runners pounding out the miles, sporting activities fill our lives. Every day, millions of fans eagerly follow the ups and the downs of their favorite teams. Professional athletes, as famous as Hollywood celebrities, peer out from television screens and billboards. A few athletes even become legends.

But not many people have what it takes to jump and spin with Charles Barkley or Kristi Yamaguchi. In fact, professional athletes are few and far between. Most people with sports careers are unsung champions—everyday folks who coach high school basketball, organize recreational activities at local community centers, and teach aerobics and tennis. This book is a behind-the-scenes tour of a dozen ways—some traditional, some not—to earn a living in the world of sports and recreation.

In the pages that follow, 12 people will take you to work. Their stories provide information about what it takes to be a sportscaster or a minor league shortstop, a sailing instructor or a college basketball coach. Some have advanced college degrees, but many learned from experience on the job. A few have known from an early age what they planned to do. Others developed their interests over time. Some are on the cutting edge of technology. Others do things the old-fashioned way. Each person and each career is different.

If you think that a sportswriter has nothing in common with an athletic trainer, think again. Although these 12 people have diverse backgrounds and interests, they have more in common than you might expect. Each person worked hard, learned skills, and acquired a knack for what he or she does. If the perfect job didn't come along at first, these people changed directions or learned new skills or volunteered their time.

Each person will tell you what they like and don't like about what they do. They have practical tips to help you explore a career in sports and recreation. Although they all work on the East Coast, you can find similar jobs all over the country.

Keep in mind, though, that these are only some of the many jobs available in the sports and recreation field. This book is not intended to provide up-to-the-minute information about salaries, new technologies, or changes in the field. That information can be found in the resources listed at the end of the book.

Twelve people. Twelve careers. Their stories may surprise you.

**Brian Ellerbe**

# Chapter One

# COLLEGE BASKETBALL COACH

I am a coach, a friend, a confidant, a doctor, a psychologist, a father, and a financial advisor," says coach Brian Ellerbe. He is describing his many roles as head coach of the men's basketball team at Loyola College in Maryland. "There are not a lot of secrets to coaching," he says. "It's all the players. They come first in every decision that is made."

Brian is among an elite few. There are only 305 head coaches in Division I of the National College Athletic Association (NCAA). Division I includes the biggest college basketball teams in the country. Smaller college teams belong to Divisions II and III.

## A Long Day

During the school year, Brian's day begins in his office at 8:30 A.M. He writes letters and makes phone calls to other coaches. He also reviews the basketball budget to make sure he hasn't spent more money on his program than the school will give him. Midmorning, he and his three assistant coaches plan the afternoon practice and discuss strategies for upcoming games.

Brian Ellerbe

**Many coaches volunteer their time in youth sports programs.**

Brian's favorite part of the day is practice. "I look forward to it," he says. "I love being around the players." He watches them closely to see which moves or plays could be improved. At the beginning of the basketball season, which lasts about six months, practices are longer and harder. By midseason, Brian is careful to make sure that team members don't practice to the point of exhaustion. Afterward, he and his assistant coaches evaluate that day's practice.

On the nights his team has a game, Brian may be interviewed by radio, television, or print journalists. A couple of evenings a week, he attends high school games to watch for future star athletes. Recruiting—attracting talented basketball players to Loyola—is an important part of Brian's job. He and his assistants visit dozens of high schools throughout the year. "To be a good coach," he says, "you have to have good people." If he attends a game or visits a recruit, his day often ends after midnight.

Summer is a little more relaxed. Recruiting continues, and Brian and his assistant coaches run summer basketball camps for Loyola students. There are also basketball tournaments. "I am planning for the following year," he says. "I try to spend some time thinking about how to use current players' skills." Like all successful coaches, Brian has a special ability for helping each player play well, individually and as part of the team.

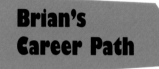

**Brian's Career Path**

"I didn't know I was going into coaching," Brian says. What he did know from a very early age is that he loved basketball. Growing up in a suburb of Washington, D.C., he attended junior and senior high schools with strong basketball programs. He credits his high

# To be a good coach, you have to have good people.

school coach with teaching him the fundamental skills of basketball.

Brian also played in the Washington summer basketball leagues from the time he was 12. He won a place on a team that competed in the national tournament of the Amateur Athletic Union, a kind of junior Olympics. "Once I got into the AAU, I felt like I was on track," he says. "I was playing with

Brian Ellerbe

Colleges, universities, and other organizations sometimes offer talented students *scholarships* to help pay for their classes, books, and living expenses.

**Coaches have to know how to play the sport they're coaching.**

15 of the best players in the Washington metro area." He knew that college basketball scouts had seen him play and that he had a good chance of going to college on a basketball scholarship.

That's exactly what happened. Rutgers University in New Jersey offered him a scholarship. He played guard on a winning team until his senior year, when he dislocated his shoulder. "It was my wake-up call," he says. "The injury changed me totally. I put the emphasis on academics." Brian studied hard while majoring in urban planning. He even did an internship with the mayor of Plainfield, New Jersey, before he graduated.

Brian's first two jobs out of college were unrelated to basketball. First he worked for a consulting company. He studied how mass transportation projects—highways, bridges, airports—affect rivers. In the fall, he returned to Washington and took a computer job tracking the federal government's fleet of vehicles.

But basketball was still on his mind. "Basketball for me is a way of life. It's like a friend," he says. He volunteered as a part-time coach for the same AAU team on which he once played. His team advanced to a regional tournament at Rutgers University. Recognizing Brian's coaching talent, Rutgers' basketball coach offered him a job as a graduate assistant coach.

Brian took the job and quickly focused again on basketball. The following season, he was hired as an assistant coach at Bowling Green University in Ohio. After two winning years, he coached at George Mason University in Virginia for a year, then moved to the University of South Carolina. Each job gave him more responsibilities and experience. Each time, his team won. Then came an assistant coaching opportunity at the University of Virginia, a Division I school with a fine basketball program. After four years, the Loyola athletic director offered Brian the head coaching job.

**Most coaches played the sport they coach.**

## Pressures of Coaching

When asked about his future, Brian responds with a laugh. "I don't look any further than where I am. You can't look ahead," he says. "Things happen so quickly." He also knows that since he was hired to develop a winning basketball program at Loyola, there is considerable pressure on him to succeed. "I don't worry about things outside of basketball," Brian says. "I would make myself nuts."

Some college sports—including Division I basketball—receive huge amounts of media

# Coaching Opportunities

There are only a few thousand college basketball coaching jobs in the country, most of them as assistants. Star college players often become coaches. The same applies to all other varsity college sports. Salaries can be very high, but jobs are stressful and demanding.

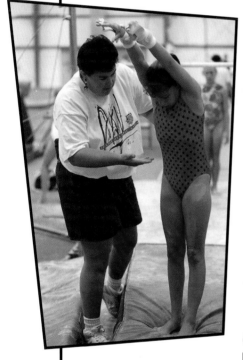

More coaching positions are available in elementary, middle, and senior high schools. "They are the heroes in coaching," says Brian, referring to high school coaches. A coach needs a college degree and state certification to teach in the public schools. Private schools have fewer requirements, but the competition for jobs may be intense.

Little League, Special Olympics, and community sports leagues also have volunteer and part-time coaching jobs available. Often neighborhood recreation programs allow older teenagers to coach younger children in sports such as volleyball, basketball, and soccer. Summer camps offer coaching opportunities, too.

coverage. Head coaches at these schools are often in the spotlight, which can be stressful. In addition, Brian says, coaches are increasingly held accountable for the actions of their players, even when they're off the court. "You are in the public eye," he says.

Brian's advice for would-be coaches? "There is no logical step or line toward coaching," he says. "You have to understand the game itself. It helps to play and have some success. You learn to think under pressure." Although he doesn't have a teaching degree, he believes one would be useful. Many college coaches first teach physical education. "The teaching side helps you communicate," he says.

Erin Miller

# Chapter Two

# Aerobics Director

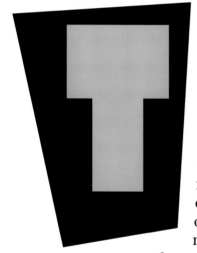

o teach aerobics, says Erin Miller, "you have to be able to think, move, and talk at the same time." During each class, she leads her students through dance and exercise routines set to music. "You have to be very clear about directions. You say it before they do it." She is constantly putting together new combinations of movements. "If it's the same thing every class, people won't come back," she says. "And you have to have fun. People come to health clubs to work out and to be with other people."

As the aerobics director for four fitness clubs in Maryland, Erin manages and trains more than 60 part-time aerobics instructors. She also teaches as many as 10 classes a week. "I love teaching," she says. "It's pretty natural for me. It's fun, not work. I couldn't sit at a desk, nine to five."

Erin Miller

## Six Days a Week

Vigorous physical exercises, called *aerobics,* build stamina by increasing the breathing and heart rates.

Erin works Monday through Saturday. She begins a typical day by teaching a 9:30 A.M. class. After each hour-long class, she spends some time with club members, then showers. By noon, she's ready to tackle her desk work: scheduling instructors, preparing the payroll, and handling suggestions from members.

"I spend a lot of time on the phone," she says. She also spends a few hours writing memos to her staff and putting together a monthly newsletter.

After a break, she teaches another class at 5:30 P.M. and leaves the club around 7 P.M. Even after a long day, her work sometimes follows her home. Evening phone calls from instructors who have scheduling problems are the one part of her job she doesn't like.

Erin also runs monthly training courses for instructors to show them new methods of teaching aerobics. Staff meetings help part-time instructors sort out scheduling problems and stay in touch. Then there are aerobics demonstrations—often at road races or health fairs—to attract business to the clubs. "We do a short five-minute routine to dance music," she says. Erin also visits each club regularly. A car phone and a laptop computer allow her to make phone calls and write reports when she is out of her office. Driving between clubs also gives her time to dream up new choreography, or dance movements, for her classes.

**Emergency Medicine Training**

When Erin graduated from the University of Maryland with a degree in emergency health services, she found there weren't any immediate openings in the area for paramedics. "Since I loved both things, fitness and emergency medicine, I decided to take whatever job came to me first," she says. She landed her aerobics job a week after graduation. "If you can get paid for

> **If you can get paid for something and have fun doing it, it's great.**

something and have fun doing it, it's great," she says.

Although Erin has worked full time for Brick Bodies Fitness Centers for less than two years, she has been teaching aerobics since she was in college. Her fitness career began when she was 16. Victor Brick— Erin's recreational basketball coach— suggested she become a trainer and help

# Careers in Fitness

Aerobic instructors and fitness trainers work in private health clubs and YMCAs or YWCAs, on cruise ships, in resorts or spas, summer camps, and corporate health centers. Personal health trainers are often self-employed and frequently make house calls.

Increasingly, fitness experts must pass a written test to be certified by the American Council on Exercise or pass written and practical tests that include teaching part of a class to be certified by the Aerobics and Fitness Association of America. Certification ensures that instructors have a background in safety and know proper teaching techniques. Most instructors learn how to teach aerobics on the job.

**A personal trainer helps a person set up a fitness program designed for his or her needs.**

members use the fitness and weight equipment. Lynne Brick, an internationally recognized instructor, taught her how to teach aerobics. While she was in college, Erin worked part time as Lynne's assistant. She learned the business side of fitness, from filling orders for exercise videos to working the front desk.

## Future of Aerobics

"Aerobics will always be around," says Erin. "It's a way people can stay healthy." She knows how hard it is for some members to stick to a fitness program. Brick Bodies Fitness Centers offer seminars on self-esteem and wellness. "We educate members about health and fitness," she says. "Most people will not be model-thin. They need to accept themselves."

*Choreography* is the sequence of moves in a dance or exercise program.

A trend Erin sees in the fitness industry is more emphasis on cross-training, or participating in more than one sport. Low-impact aerobics, which are easier on the body, are also popular. And more classes are available for kids or the elderly. Each group has special needs and special strengths.

"An aerobics instructor always has to work part time," says Erin. "You can't teach aerobics 40 hours a week." Most instructors have other full-time jobs, such as teaching in a school. And although many fitness clubs have an aerobics director, that person may only work part time if the club is small.

By *cross-training,* or playing more than one sport, athletes develop all their muscles without overusing or harming any one muscle.

Erin suggests that people who want to teach aerobics join a health club. "See what classes are like," she says. "Take kids' aerobics classes. You must enjoy moving.

Try to play team sports." She also recommends dance classes, which emphasize rhythm and movement. It helps to have an ear for music. Erin chooses fitness tapes that have a certain number of beats per minute. Hip-hop, funk, African, and Latin rhythms are among her favorites.

"It's important to be able to lead others. You have to feel comfortable leading and public speaking," she says. "You have to enjoy people and be able to accept criticism." Erin also handles members' complaints about the aerobics program. Some people want different music or more advanced movements or clearer instructions. "You are dealing with different kinds of people," she says. "You can't please everybody."

In addition, many of the part-time instructors she trains and evaluates are older and more experienced than she is. They may feel offended that someone younger, with less experience, is supervising them. "If we have a problem, I have to handle it delicately," Erin says.

"My job responsibilities here will grow as we add more clients," Erin says. She expects to eventually turn to a medical career, perhaps returning to school to become a physician's assistant.

Gerry Sandusky

# Chapter Three

# TV SPORTSCASTER

ach weekday evening at 6:20 P.M., sportscaster Gerry Sandusky is beamed into 70,000 Baltimore homes. His time on camera is the high point of his day. "It's like flying a plane. There's an elevated feel to it," he says. At 11:20 P.M., he does the late sports news for television station WBAL. Sportscasting often looks effortless, even glamorous. What Gerry's audience doesn't realize is the amount of pre-broadcast preparation the job requires. Working out of a cramped, windowless office beneath the television studio, he spends hours choosing stories and writing his scripts. Gerry also does his own live on-air reporting, covering important games or events and taping interviews with sports personalities. He also works closely with his full-time producer, who keeps him up-to-date on stories that are happening during the show. Gerry needs his help to create visuals such as charts and graphs, and to find and edit videotapes. "Everyone gets to see you for four or five, maybe eight minutes, each night," he says. "But for every minute on the air, there's an hour of preparation time."

Gerry Sanduski

## Hulk Hogan and Babe Ruth

Although a typical day for Gerry usually begins at 2 or 3 P.M., today he arrives early to interview professional wrestler Hulk Hogan. "I think: 'What's the angle on Hulk Hogan?'" he says. Instead of the usual questions about Hulk's wrestling career, Gerry decides to ask about his kids. "We got a picture of this man-eating wrestler who turns out to be a tender father."

Back at the station, Gerry scans his computer for the main sports stories of the day. His station has satellite hookups with NBC and CNN. "I see what material I have to work with," he says. He will open the sports news with his lead, the story that he considers to be the most newsworthy and interesting to viewers in Baltimore.

By 4:30 P.M., Gerry is writing his script and working with his producer to arrange the order of the stories in the sports segment. They choose videotape from the satellite feeds, from footage WBAL photographers have shot at local sports events, or from the station's archives. At 5 P.M., he goes over the final script, watching for breaking news. Sometimes an entire segment is discarded because of a late story. "What has taken all afternoon, we then do in 15 minutes," he says, half-joking about how fast they must edit a late-breaking story. At 5:45, Gerry, like all broadcasters, puts on makeup to look better for the camera. It's a skill he taught himself.

After the 6 P.M. show and dinner, Gerry goes back to work. "I start all over again for

**Very bright lights are used when filming TV shows. The lights can make people look funny, with harsh shadows or shiny faces. Sportscasters and other people who appear on television wear makeup so they look better under the hot lights.**

the 11 P.M. show, asking myself what is still newsworthy." At 11:20 he is on the air again. Before leaving the station around 12:30 A.M., he tapes a sportscast for the morning show.

**Football Fan**

Gerry's favorite sport is football. That's not surprising since his father is John Sandusky, who played for the Cleveland Browns and the Green Bay Packers, and later coached the Baltimore Colts (now in Indianapolis), the Philadelphia Eagles, and the Miami Dolphins. Although Gerry spent his summers as a teenager working at NFL training camps—taking care of equipment, doing laundry, getting water—he never dreamed about playing professional football. "By the time I was 10, I knew I wasn't fast enough or big enough," he says.

# Shows are never as good as you think or as bad as you think.

Instead, Gerry played football and basketball for fun in high school in Florida, then at Towson State University in Maryland. After earning a bachelor's degree in business and finance, he realized that he didn't want to work for a bank or an insurance company. Returning to Florida, he volunteered as an intern at television station WSVN in Miami.

"At first I just watched everybody," he

**Broadcasters need good computer skills.**

Documents and videotapes are stored in an *archive* or library.

says. Soon he had learned how to produce a television segment by choosing, editing, and assembling stories. After six months, Gerry began earning an hourly wage. He was then offered a full-time job. "I split my time between producing for other sportscasters and reporting feature stories." He stayed at WSVN for six years, becoming a full-time reporter and then the weekend sportscaster. In 1988, WBAL in Baltimore hired him to do the 11 P.M. sports.

Gerry is now the sports director. Along with that title he has many behind-the-scenes responsibilities. He arranges for the credentials or identification passes reporters and camera operators need to get into sports events or games. He also plans future sports stories and coordinates WBAL's coverage of such special events as the Olympic Games. Helping Gerry are his full-time producer, a part-time producer, and WBAL's student interns.

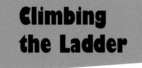

# Climbing the Ladder

"The traditional path to become a sportscaster is to go to college to study television production and communications," says Gerry. "Then you begin in a small town in a part of the country you've never heard of. You climb the ladder." Since he learned his technical skills on the job as an intern, Gerry has created the WBAL Sports Internship Program to give others the same opportunity. More than 60 students at local colleges have earned college credit by interning at WBAL.

Along with technical knowledge of video and audio equipment, sportscasters must learn to use an IFB, or Interruptive Feedback, an earpiece that they wear to hear their producers during broadcasts. The IFB makes it possible for Gerry's producer to give him late news. When he is reporting live from an event, his producer uses the IFB to let him know of technical problems. "Your mouth is on autopilot," Gerry says. "It takes a lot of getting used to."

Then there is pre-broadcast stage fright. Gerry recalls his first broadcast. "I was hoping that the world would end." As it turned out, the Super Bowl was being televised on another channel. "Nobody was watching me anyway," he says. "Shows are never as good as you think or as bad as you think." Within a year, his fear tapered off.

# Sportscasting's Future

"There will always be more people than jobs," Gerry says, referring to full-time, paid sportscasting positions. "Internships are important," he says. Self-confidence, flexibility, grace under pressure, and an "unquenchable thirst for information" are all vital to a sportscaster. "It's important to have

# Sports Careers in Television

A sportscaster works with photographers, engineers, stage managers, and other behind-the-scenes employees. A sports segment producer works closely with the sportscaster. He or she needs not only the technical skills to assemble a story, but knowledge about a wide variety of sports.

Gerry's producer is a graduate of the WBAL Sports Internship Program. At many stations, the weekend sportscaster may also pinch-hit as an on-the-scene reporter during the week.

Sportscasters are frequently paid well. Salaries are related to the size of the station and the sportscaster's years of experience. Most sportscasters and reporters work under legal contracts that cover a specific period of time and pay level. At the end of the time period, contracts are either renegotiated or dropped. Producers can be employees of the station or work under contract. Some work part time.

**Television and radio reporters talk to athletes right after games.**

confidence in your uniqueness," he says. His advice is to stay focused on your dreams.

Gerry recommends that future broadcasters "read about sports, watch sports, go to sporting events, learn the players, and learn the games. And try to play some of the games. You don't have to be good. The experience will make you less inclined to be critical."

Gerry does the "color commentary"—background about the game and sport rather than the play-by-play description—for the University of Maryland football games on radio. He would like to announce more games on the radio. "You're in the game," he says. "It's unfolding. There are no scripts."

Suzanne Sanders

# Chapter Four

# ATHLETIC TRAINER

**B**eing an athletic trainer is like being a detective," says Suzanne Sanders. "You figure out what's causing the problem and ways to solve it." As a certified athletic trainer, she works with members of several varsity teams at Towson State University to prevent and treat injuries. "We try to keep the athletes in a condition to be able to play safely," she says. "This is a fun profession. The athletes are motivated. I like seeing them get better."

There are rewards for being an athletic trainer, but there are also frustrations. Athletes, she says, often try to ignore injuries. "They are afraid we'll pull them out of their sports, although our goal is their health," she says. She handles everything from cuts and bruises to

Suzanne Sanders

"overuse" or repetitive motion injuries that occur when an athlete trains too hard. "When they're getting worse, they come in to see me and want me to cure them instantly," she says. By that time, Suzanne may have to restrict their practice or playing. This can sometimes lead to conflicts with coaches or the athletes themselves, particularly before an important game or meet.

## The Training Room

Suzanne is in the university's training room— with its exercise equipment, whirlpools, and treatment tables—from 12:30 to 6:30 P.M., Monday through Friday. She also comes in on weekends to be on hand for games.

On a typical day, Suzanne meets with members of the swimming and basketball teams. She checks each injury individually, then recommends treatments. She uses heat or ice, electrical stimulation of the muscles, or ultrasound therapy to reduce pain and swelling. "I assess if the injury is better or worse. I also determine if someone can practice fully or whether training is limited," she says.

Suzanne also treats new injuries. For a swimmer with a sore shoulder, she asks how the injury happened, observes the woman's movements, then palpates, or touches, the shoulder. She also checks muscle strength, comparing the injured side of the body to the uninjured side. "I check for pain and strength and to determine which motions are problems. I ask about her practice. I try to decide what is wrong with her and put her on appropriate treatment." Suzanne might also suggest a strengthening and stretching program.

After talking with an athlete, Suzanne gives the coach a list of recommendations. She estimates that she spends about 30 percent of her time at her desk. "We do a lot of paperwork," she says, referring to the daily record keeping of each athlete's progress. She also enters medical records from family doctors into the computer and sees that insurance forms are completed.

## A Tomboy

"I grew up with brothers. I was a tomboy," Suzanne says, recalling her childhood. She played tennis and softball. After graduating from high school, she worked for a year at a tennis shop. Then she enrolled at West Virginia Wesleyan College to pursue a

# This is a fun profession.

physical education major. "I was injured playing tennis and ended up in the training room," she remembers. Although her sprained ankle wasn't serious, she became interested in sports medicine and worked as an unpaid student trainer. Her duties were similar to those she now performs, although she worked under a certified trainer. At Towson State, she now supervises student trainers.

**Trainers tape athletes and help them ice sore or injured parts of their bodies.**

After college, Suzanne taught physical education in a private school, sold gifts in a shop, and trained as a bank teller. Each job was a little less satisfying than the one before it. Fed up with work that had no meaning for her, she enrolled at Towson State to work toward a second bachelor's degree with the goal of becoming a certified athletic trainer.

As a student trainer, Suzanne clocked 2,000 hours of clinical, or practical, experience. She also traveled with Towson State's teams. "Travel entails a lot of responsibility," she says, "because, except for

# Becoming a Certified Athletic Trainer

There are two routes to becoming a certified athletic trainer. The first is to earn a degree in an accredited graduate or undergraduate athletic training program at a college or university. The second is to get a bachelor's degree in another major and work a minimum of 1,500 hours in an internship program under a certified trainer.

Since trainers are health professionals, they study anatomy, physiology, and kinesiology, or the biology of movement. Practical courses teach them how to tape and wrap body parts, such as ankles, to limit movement, work with athletes for overall fitness, and prevent injuries  through preseason screening. In addition, trainers take courses in injury evaluation and emergency or first-aid procedures. To be certified, trainers must pass a written, practical, and oral exam given by the National Athletic Trainers' Association.

Trainers work in colleges and universities, high schools, sports medicine clinics, corporate health programs, health clubs, and for professional sports teams. High-pressure jobs with professional teams pay the highest salaries.

Suzanne Sanders

A *physical therapist* has more medical training than an athletic trainer. Some physical therapists specialize in treating sports injuries. Like athletic trainers, they may use massage, exercise, or heat.

football, you travel without a certified trainer." After graduation, she passed the certification exam.

Suzanne also works two mornings a week at a sports medicine clinic as a physical therapy technician. After a physical therapist makes the diagnosis for a patient, Suzanne oversees the patient's rehabilitation and exercise programs, using many of the same treatments she uses with her university athletes.

Although Suzanne is a certified trainer, she is also a graduate student at Towson State working on a master's degree in human resources management. Her program focuses on program development and job counseling—skills she believes may be useful later in her career. Towson State employs Suzanne under a graduate assistantship, which helps her to pay for her education and living expenses. When she finishes her degree, she plans to look for a permanent job as a trainer at another college.

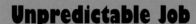

## Unpredictable Job

"I've gotten better at my communication skills," Suzanne says. "I have to speak to physicians and coaches and handle conflicts without taking it personally." Patience, tolerance of many types of personalities, and the ability to handle surprises are essential for a trainer. "It's not a predictable job," she says. She remembers the time a weight lifter, lying on his back with a 250-pound weight overhead, lost control and dropped it on his face. After calling 911, the trainers monitored his blood pressure and heart rate until help arrived. He required 14 hours of reconstructive surgery.

Suzanne advises trainers-to-be to assist a certified trainer in high school if possible. Taking first-aid courses from the American Red Cross and learning about many different sports are also good steps.

What's the outlook for athletic trainers? Suzanne believes that, as more and more states require high schools to hire athletic trainers to be at games, the number of jobs will increase.

**K e n   A r n o l d**

# Chapter Five

# SHORTSTOP

hortstop Ken Arnold knows he may never play major league baseball. He plays for the Winnipeg (Canada) Goldeyes in the independent Northern League. He joined the Northern League after playing for several years with the Baltimore Orioles' Class AA team in Bowie, Maryland. In April 1995, he was abruptly released from his contract with the Bowie Baysox. "Baseball is a big business," Ken says. "You can be released in the blink of an eye."

Major league baseball develops new players through its "farm system." Each team supports minor league teams to find and train talented young players. Many players climb the baseball ladder from Rookie, to Class A, to Class AA, and finally Class AAA baseball—the level just before the majors. Players work under contract and may be traded like major leaguers. Teams in independent leagues, such as the Northern League, are not part of major league baseball or any "farm system." But they are still professional teams, that is, the players are paid to play baseball.

Why does Ken play professional baseball? "It ain't the money," he jokes. "But when I go to the field, little kids look up and want my autograph. I love playing. I'm going to keep doing it until they drag me off the field."

## A Day in the Minors

During baseball season, a day on the road with a minor or independent league team begins early. Sometimes, the bus leaves at 7 A.M. "There are tough bus rides," he says. "You play a lot of Scrabble and cards and watch a lot of movies."

At practice, usually in the afternoon, players stretch for 20 minutes and then throw for another 20 minutes. Then they take batting practice. Fielding practice follows. Players get dressed in their game uniforms and grab a snack before the game starts. Most night games last until about 10 P.M.

The next day, the travel routine begins all over again. "It's tough when you have to play the next day," says Ken. "At home, it's a little easier. But when we're not on the road, there are early workouts and extra batting and infield practice." Road trips last for as long as 10 days. And during the baseball season—April to September—there are few days off.

## A Big Family

The players travel with their manager, trainers, coaches, and a publicity person. "It's like a big family," says Ken. "You don't have to like a guy, but you'd better be able to turn a double play with him." A sense of humor helps him get along with others. "You can be too uptight. It's

going to affect the way you play."

Professional players are always under pressure to play well, in order to keep their jobs and please their fans. "I tell myself I'm out there to have fun," he says. "If I make a mistake, it's all right." Ken also believes that the pressure isn't all bad. "Internal pressure is one of the things that makes you keep going," he says. "It's part of the competitiveness. I don't like to lose."

## An Academic Scholarship

Ken grew up in New Jersey playing Little League baseball. In high school, he played baseball, basketball, and football while getting grades good enough to qualify for the

> **I tell myself I'm out there to have fun. If I make a mistake, it's all right.**

National Honor Society. Armed with an academic scholarship, he headed for Wagner College in New York with plans to study business administration. He remembers the athletic director's words after watching him play: "I think you have a future playing baseball." The head baseball coach soon became his mentor, or teacher. "He was a father away from home," says Ken.

# Playing Professionally

Although there is no direct route to a professional sports career—whether it be in baseball, golf, tennis, hockey, basketball, or football—most successful athletes play their sports from an early age with total commitment. Only highly motivated and superbly talented players need apply.

A few athletes—Michael Jordan, Cal Ripken, Martina Navratilova, Steve Young—earn millions and become stars. Most do not. Salaries for players on the lower rungs of the professional sports ladder are often low. Ken made barely enough to live on during his rookie year with the Chicago Cubs. He supported himself by substitute teaching and working as a waiter during the off-season.

Steve Young, quarterback of the San Francisco 49ers, is one of the lucky few who make a living playing professional football.

The summer before his senior year, Ken's coach recommended him for a place in the Collegiate League in upstate New York. Colleges send their best players to the Collegiate League so that they can be seen by major league scouts. Both the Chicago Cubs and the Minnesota Twins were interested in Ken, and the Twins said they would draft him. When they didn't, Ken returned to Wagner College. In the last game of the fall at Wagner, he injured his knee and underwent two surgeries to repair the damage. Convinced that his professional baseball career was over before it had begun, Ken accepted an offer from Wagner to become an assistant coach.

But the Chicago Cubs had plans for Ken. In June, they drafted him for the Rookie League Huntington Cubs in West Virginia. Despite

A *scout* seeks promising athletes for a team.

**Not many hockey players make it to the top level of professional hockey— the National Hockey League. There are other professional and semi-professional leagues.**

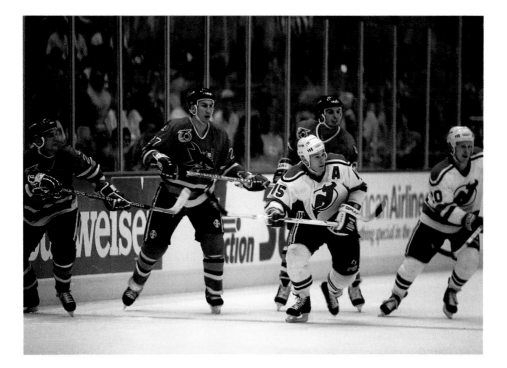

**Professional beach volleyball has become a popular sport for women and men. Two-player teams compete in professional tournaments in California, Hawaii, Florida, and New Jersey.**

another knee injury and more surgery, he made the Rookie League All-Star team. His second year—with the Cubs' AA club, the Peoria Chiefs—didn't go as well. "Nine games into the season, I broke my hand and got hit in the throat," Ken says. His .280 batting average dropped to .210. During spring training the following season, he was released from his contract with the Cubs. "It was the longest day of my life," he says.

Shocked at first, Ken quickly recovered. He flew to California for tryouts for the independent Northern League. He won a spot with the Thunder Bay Whiskeyjacks in Canada. After a great season, in which he was chosen Player of the Year, Ken was traded to the Baltimore Orioles. He played 83 games and batted .270 for the Baysox. When he was released from his contract with the Bowie Baysox in the spring of 1995, he became a free agent.

## A Baseball Gym

Although Ken is hopeful about continuing to play baseball professionally, he is also practical. He has written a business plan and found investors for a baseball gym—complete with batting cage and weight room—which he plans to open near his New Jersey home. Coaching baseball at all levels is another interest of his.

Ken's advice if you want to play professionally is to play Little League and high school baseball. He also recommends going to baseball camps. "If you're determined to do it, give it your best shot," he says. "And get as much education as you can. You never know when it [baseball playing] is going to end."

A professional athlete who is not under contract with any team is a *free agent.* An athlete under contract to a team may be traded. When that contract expires, the athlete becomes a free agent.

**Brenda Gilmore**

# Chapter Six

# School Program Director

**A**s a school program director for the U.S. Tennis Association (USTA), Brenda Gilmore introduces tennis to students in Maryland, Washington, D.C., and Virginia. "Basically I'm a salesperson selling tennis," she says. "I'm trying to get tennis as popular as basketball, baseball, and football." Then she laughs. "If I do a really good job, I'll put myself out of a job. We won't need anyone to promote tennis any more."

Although Brenda has always been athletic, she never imagined she'd be promoting tennis. Her career in photography was in high gear when a car accident left her in a wheelchair. She took a job in the photography department of the Smithsonian Institution's Museum of American History after the accident, and began playing wheelchair tennis to keep active. Then she won a tournament. "I got a trophy and I was hooked," she says.

Brenda Gilmore

## 140,000 Miles

Brenda spends a large part of her time conducting training programs for physical education teachers throughout the mid-Atlantic region. "I show instructors how to turn a gym or parking lot into a tennis court," she says. She also demonstrates wheelchair tennis to the students at school assemblies. "This is more gratifying than any trophy I have ever won."

She spends as many as three days a week visiting schools. A typical day might mean a four-hour drive from her home in Maryland to Virginia Beach for an afternoon presentation. After staying overnight, she returns to her office to handle her paperwork and phone calls. Her day often ends with an evening committee meeting. It can be an exhausting schedule. "I did 140,000 miles in less than five years," she says.

Brenda now spends more time in the office and less in her car. She trains other tennis professionals—called clinicians—to conduct school programs in her place. Although she technically works from nine to five, Monday through Friday, she also gives tennis clinics or makes presentations on Saturdays and Sundays. Organizing teacher-training programs, writing reports and articles for a newsletter, and planning special events take a big chunk of her time. These events include the USTA's annual meeting or Hall of Fame dinner, where she often handles the registration desk.

Brenda also attends many committee meetings. The USTA is run by volunteer committee members who hire full-time staffers to manage the programs. Each program is governed by a committee. The school program committee oversees Brenda's work.

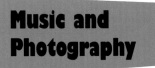

## Music and Photography

Brenda's first love was singing. She planned to study music at Howard University in Washington, D.C., but soon discovered she was more interested in jazz than classical music. She switched to a major in technical theater, taking courses in film and television,

> " If I do a really good job, I'll put myself out of a job. We won't need anyone to promote tennis any more. "

stage lighting, and drama. And she discovered photography. "I liked it and I was good at it," she says. She earned money by taking yearbook and fraternity pictures.

After graduation, Brenda returned to her hometown of New York City to work in the theater and at a television station. Back in Washington a year later, she took a job processing prints at a photo laboratory. That job led her to freelance photography assignments and the job at the Smithsonian.

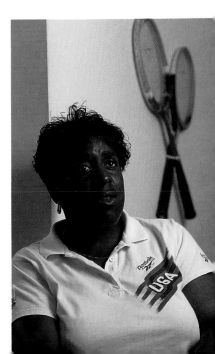

# Camp Counselors

A summer job as a camp counselor is one way to get paid experience in a recreational field. Many day and overnight camps hire teenagers who are juniors in high school to assist with sports activities or to be counselors for younger children.

YMCAs and local recreation centers also conduct day camps and summer programs. Some offer training for interested teens. In addition, some camps feature certain sports or cater to children with special needs such as physical handicaps. Working as a lifeguard or a swimming instructor is another option.

Camp counselors often need experience in a variety of individual and team sports, references from teachers or coaches, and first aid, lifeguard, and water safety training certificates from the American Red Cross. Counselors who teach boating may need to be "dinghy" certified by the U.S. Sailing Association. Pay for camp counselors is often low. School and community libraries and the American Camping Association can provide directories of camps.

**Camp counselors organize activities for young campers.**

Then came the car accident. "Before that, I would ride my bike to work and jog," she says. "Now I needed to find some kind of activity I could get involved in."

Tennis was the answer. "I went to a match and found people in wheelchairs who played well," she says. After playing and taking lessons for five years, Brenda resigned from the Smithsonian Institution to play full time on the wheelchair tennis circuit. Her professional career lasted three years. Although she was ranked third in the country, her dream of finding a sponsor to support what she calls her "tennis habit" never came true. When her money ran low, she supported herself by designing and selling T-shirts.

Brenda was recruited as a volunteer on the USTA Education Committee. Her volunteer work led to an offer of part-time work. She accepted her current job a few months later.

**Computers make administrative tasks, such as compiling membership lists, fundraising, and writing, a little easier.**

Brenda Gilmore

Brenda is now focusing on finding new ways to involve community leaders, parents, and physical education teachers in the USTA tennis programs. She plans to organize special events and speak at more community and school meetings. She also volunteers, coaches and does administrative work as the executive director of a community tennis program in the suburban Maryland county where she lives.

## Necessary Skills

"I've grown tremendously in the four years I've been here," Brenda says of her job at the USTA. She has learned to manage her time and communicate better. "My theater training helped a lot," she says.

Brenda uses her writing and teaching abilities every day. She has learned to work with others in committees. "There are a lot more things I need to learn about running an organization," she says. "And you can't exist without using a computer. Every six months there's something new." She uses graphics, database, word processing, and spreadsheet software.

"Jobs in associations are hard to get," she says. Although there are sports associations that govern all amateur and professional sports, most are small, with few staff positions. Competition for jobs is fierce. If you want to work with an association, Brenda suggests you start in your area. Most local sports teams or leagues need volunteers.

# Sports Management

Lawyers play an increasingly large role in the world of sports. "Sports management is a big field," Brenda says. "And it's going to grow tremendously." Not only do all sports associations hire attorneys, but lawyers work as agents for players or as representatives for the owners of professional teams. A law degree is necessary. To be licensed to practice, lawyers must pass the American Bar Association exam in their state. Attorneys, particularly agents, often make high salaries, but the work can be stressful with long hours.

Mike Woodard

# Chapter Seven

# SPORTS FACILITY MANAGER

ou don't have to know soccer to run this place," says facility manager Mike Woodard. "The big thing is organization and planning. This is a business. The soccer is a bonus." He strides through the large indoor soccer arena overlooking Baltimore's harbor. A fraying seam in the green artificial turf catches his attention. "In July and August we do maintenance on the building that we can't do the rest of the year," he says.

As manager of the Clarence "Du" Burns Arena—named for a former mayor of Baltimore—Mike is responsible for the upkeep of the building and for organizing 300 soccer teams into leagues. Three professional teams—the Baltimore Spirit and the Baltimore Bays, both soccer clubs, and the Baltimore Thunder, an indoor lacrosse team—use the arena for practice. On Friday evenings, the Bays also play home games here, to crowds that fill the arena's 650 seats.

Mike Woodard

"We're open seven days a week, 8 A.M. through midnight," says Mike. "I'm a good organizer, but it's a lot to run."

## A Lot of Paperwork

As an employee of Baltimore's City Recreation and Parks Department, Mike works Monday through Friday and weekends during soccer tournaments. A typical day begins at noon and ends about 8 P.M.

Three-quarters of his time is spent handling the avalanche of contracts, forms, and questionnaires that cover his desk. He sets up leagues, schedules games, writes brochures, calculates league statistics, and coordinates practice time with the professional teams that use the facility.

Mike also makes food and entertainment arrangements for Halloween, Christmas, and Easter parties for neighborhood children. He keeps track of the money spent on the arena, orders supplies and equipment, checks the building's security system, and oversees any repairs and improvements. "In sports," he says cheerfully, "there is a lot of paperwork."

A computer, its screen blinking, sits at the side of his desk. "This has helped me immensely," he says. "I do a lot of writing." In addition to a word processing program, he uses spreadsheet software to manage the budget. He uses graphics programs to design brochures, make signs, and produce the arena's calendar of events. The computer helps him keep track of which teams have signed up for leagues and tournaments.

Mike supervises a full-time secretary and the part-time maintenance person who does routine cleaning. In addition, he has trained 16 part-time sports coordinators who run programs when he is not there. "They have to be very dependable," he says. "The sports coordinators are here to supervise the building and take phone calls." Mike calls staff meetings to discuss upcoming programs and ways to handle paperwork and problems.

Then there are the constant phone calls. A beeper attached to Mike's belt gets his attention when he is not at his desk. "You need a lot of flexibility," he says. "There are a lot of interruptions. I like it because there are a lot of things going on."

There are also frustrations. Since Mike works for the city of Baltimore, he sometimes gets discouraged when strict government rules and regulations limit the improvements he can make at the arena.

# "In sports, there is a lot of paperwork."

## The Sweeper

After playing soccer, basketball, and baseball during high school, Mike headed for the University of Maryland to study history and play more soccer. "I played sweeper, the last one defensively before the goalie," he says.

Mike's career with the Recreation and Parks Department began when he was in college. As a part-time recreation aide in a community center, he coached and organized soccer and softball leagues, scheduled and refereed games, and booked the umpires. Within a couple of years, he was offered a full-time job as a recreation leader.

The job brought him to a crossroads: should he continue with his history major or transfer to another college where he could study recreation? His soccer coach suggested he stay with history and get his Maryland state teaching certification. "It was great advice. I loved teaching," he says. He now teaches physical education classes two mornings a week in a church school.

Mike continued working for the Recreation and Parks Department after college, transferring to the Myers Pavilion, another soccer arena in Baltimore. He was soon promoted to recreation director. When the "Du" Burns Arena opened in 1990, Mike operated both facilities until he was assigned full time to the new arena.

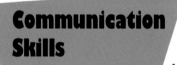

## Communication Skills

Mike's success in managing a sports center is directly related to his skill in handling people. Coaches and individuals who have missed deadlines to sign up for soccer leagues have to be turned away with fairness and tact. "It's public relations," says Mike. "People sometimes get in a big huff, but you have to handle them."

There are also hot tempers to deal with when players and coaches believe a referee has made a bad call. Mike tries to be fair.

# Officiating at Games

The requirements for sports officials vary depending on the sport. Officials are needed at all levels, from professional sports to neighborhood leagues. Professional organizations for each sport train and hire their own officials. Although most training is handled locally, seminars and workshops for officials are also held regionally or nationally. Some officials, such as baseball umpires, go to school to learn their trade. Others must pass practical and written tests given by national associations.

To be an official—at any level—you need to know the basic rules of the sport. You also need a level head, a decisive manner, and the ability to handle conflict.

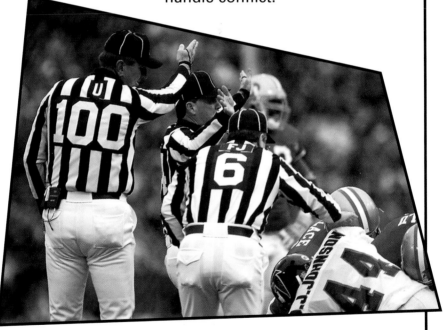

"I'm sensitive to both sides," he says. "I've been an official, a coach, and a player. There is always grumbling, but no major blowouts." He doesn't tolerate violence. When two amateur players were caught fighting after a game, he pulled them apart and suspended both for the rest of the season. "I've gotten better at dealing with people," he says, "although I was always pretty good at it."

## The Business of Recreation

The future of sports facility management jobs, Mike believes, will be at commercial facilities, such as skating and roller rinks, swimming pools, and private health clubs. He recommends getting a business or management degree. "This is a business," he says. "You need to deal with budgets and the bottom line." Volunteering at a neighborhood recreation center—coaching or setting up leagues—is a way to get experience.

As for his future, Mike says, "I'm happy with what I'm doing." He hopes, however, to do more creative summer programs. "I'd love to do events like wrestling and boxing or concerts," he says. Because the arena needs air conditioning and a new sound system, he knows new programs will require fund-raising and careful planning.

Jane Harkaway

# Chapter Eight

# SPECIAL OLYMPICS ADMINISTRATOR

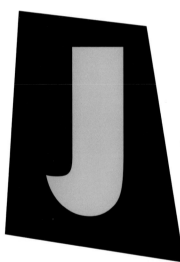

J ane Harkaway's official title is a mouthful: adaptive physical education resource teacher and county director of Special Olympics. The Special Olympics is an international program for handicapped athletes. "I figure out how to accommodate children with special problems," she says. She also finds ways for students who are mentally retarded, physically handicapped, emotionally disturbed, deaf, or blind to participate in regular physical education classes.

"It's very challenging to come up with things to make sure a kid is included," says Jane. "It's what I like about my job." In a volleyball class, for example, she might attach a beach ball to the net or use a lighter-weight ball. A child with special needs who cannot hit a regular volleyball can often hit other balls instead. "Often their muscles don't work," she says. "The key is balance and strength and special awareness." Then she smiles, remembering one boy who

Jane Harkaway

learned to play volleyball. "He just lit up. I love to watch kids light up," Jane says.

**Many Meetings**

Jane divides her time between the county's Special Olympics program and the schools. She visits more than 100 schools. Besides her standard 8 A.M. to 3:30 P.M. work hours, she coaches Special Olympics athletes in basketball, softball, aquatics, or skiing two evenings a week.

During a school visit, Jane talks first with a physical education teacher or physical therapist. Then she reads the student's record

for clues to problems. Finally, she meets the child who needs assistance in gym class. "I figure out how best to help," she says. Since children sometimes act up, her job can be frustrating. "Even if someone is driving you up a wall," she says, "you have to be kind."

On days when she has no school visits, Jane returns phone calls and completes reports about students. She also writes a newsletter to inform Special Olympics coaches of coming events, orders uniforms or special equipment, organizes trips for Special Olympics athletes, and attends meetings. "Unfortunately, I have to attend a lot of meetings," she groans. "People talk on and on. What could have been done in an hour takes a day."

# You are the one who gives. You get rewarded in different ways.

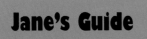

Jane's work is rooted in her past. Her youngest brother had mental retardation and was a Special Olympics athlete. "I don't think I would have known about special needs and sensitivity unless I had him as a guide," she says.

In high school, Jane was certified as a water safety instructor and a lifeguard by the American Red Cross, and worked as a lifeguard in community pools. She majored

# Opportunities in Physical Education

Physical education (P.E.) teachers work in public, private, and parochial—or church—schools, and in colleges and universities. Almost all teaching jobs require at least a bachelor's degree, with a major in physical education. Many P.E. teachers also coach.

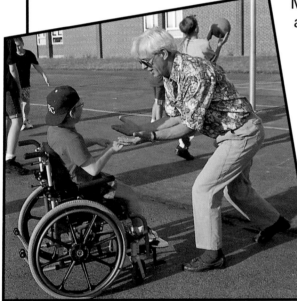

To teach in a public school, a P.E. teacher must be certified by the state. Each state has particular requirements, including education courses, tests, and student teaching experience. To teach at a university, you need at least a master's degree, often a doctoral degree. Depending on the state, teachers who work with students with special needs or who want to become school principals need additional education or degrees.

**Physical education teachers teach students lifelong health habits.**

in physical education at the University of
Maryland. During summers in college, she
taught swimming and worked as a recreation
assistant for people with special needs. For
one of her college courses, she taught a girl
with cerebral palsy how to swim, then bike
and walk.

After graduation, Jane taught physical
education in a private school, then
transferred to a public school for emotionally
disturbed children. Ready for a change, she
moved to California and managed an aquatics
program at a country club. Then came a

**Special Olympics
meets give people
with disabilities the
chance to compete.
Other people can help
by coaching the
Special Olympians
and cheering for
them.**

bombshell. Jane had developed Hodgkin's disease, which is cancer of the lymph system. She returned to Maryland for treatment.

Within a year, Jane was feeling well enough to take a summer job coaching and teaching retarded children. It became a full-time position, teaching overactive boys, 9 to 12 years old. "They were my wild boys," she says with affection. She also took the courses necessary to get her special education certificate. Eager to go back to teaching physical education, she took a job on Maryland's Eastern Shore.

After two years, Jane accepted a job teaching retarded children how to move and walk. She also began a Special Olympics program. A year later, she transferred to a special center where she taught special education students to do work, such as kitchen and janitorial chores, gardening, and stuffing envelopes. Studying part time, Jane completed a master's degree in education from Bowie State College. Three years ago, she was offered her current job.

Although she enjoys what she does, Jane is ready for new challenges. "I'd like to be the principal of a school," she says. To qualify, she plans to take more courses to prepare for the supervisor administration certificate that Maryland schools require of principals.

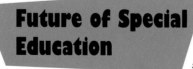

## Future of Special Education

Jane predicts that more people will do her type of work in the future. "We are getting more children with special needs," she says, which she thinks is because of increased drug use. She offers this advice to those thinking of a career in special education: "Have patience, be flexible, be tolerant. You are the one who gives. You get rewarded in different ways."

Getting involved in volunteer organizations such as Girl Scouts or Little League Challenger is also a good idea, Jane says. Students in their mid-teens are welcomed as volunteer coaches with Special Olympics athletes. "And in your own school, be a friend to special kids," she says. "Find out that they are like you."

Peter Martin

# Chapter Nine

# NATURALIST

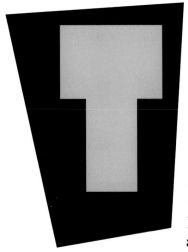

The outdoor activities you may enjoy in your spare time are Peter Martin's work. As the senior naturalist for the Irvine Natural Science Center, he creates nature programs for people of all ages, often leading nature and bird walks on the trails that wind through the woods and fields north of Baltimore. He also teaches natural science courses and helps plan the summer camp program.

Peter worries that many children have little contact with nature. "We're trying to get younger kids to use their senses," he says. During nature walks, for example, he shows children how to look under leaves with a magnifying glass or search tree trunks for salamanders, snails, or slug eggs. "We teach people how to experience their surroundings, but we want them to have a good time," he says. "I feel really good when I feel that people come away having learned something."

Following the Seasons

Peter's schedule is dictated by the seasons. In fall and spring he conducts daily nature walks. Participants look for birds nesting

Peter Martin

and mating, and, using binoculars, try to identify migrating species. He researches the subject for each walk, then writes an outline. To prepare for a Furry Animal Walk, for example, he might spend a couple of hours on the trail looking for tracks and droppings. "Scouting work takes time," he says. Although Peter usually works from eight or nine in the morning until four or five in the afternoon, morning and evening programs can make for an occasional 12- or 14-hour day.

Part of each day, Peter develops new programs. He reads nature magazines and activity books for ideas. "You have to be creative," he says. He teaches people how to make Christmas ornaments out of acorns, seed heads, wildflowers, and weeds. In another course, children learn to make musical instruments—drums and rattles— using seeds, pods, and pine cones. "I have to collect those things," he says. He spends

about 40 percent of his time conducting field trips and teaching, and another 30 percent preparing for the field trips and classes.

Peter spends the rest of his day scheduling school field trips, writing letters and articles for the center's newsletter, and mailing brochures and registration forms. He also trains volunteers and gives natural science lectures to garden club members.

Summers are no less busy. Day camps, with hikes and fishing trips, last for a week or two. To teach children about the natural world, Peter organizes scavenger hunts or games. In one game called Survival, children assume the roles of predators, herbivores,

# We teach people how to experience their surroundings, but we want them to have a good time.

and omnivores searching for food. Animals who are not successful become extinct. A Native American game called Double Ball— a game of catch played with two bean bags thrown between wooden sticks—is a fun way to learn about native culture. "To help younger kids, you need to be animated and silly," Peter says. "I'm an entertainer. I have to be pumped up."

Peter also runs overnight camping trips for

older children. Campfire programs include games, music, and outdoor meals. Past groups have visited wildlife refuges near the Chesapeake Bay on Maryland's Eastern Shore. Peter is planning a trip to Hawk Mountain Sanctuary in southern Pennsylvania to view the hawk migration. "Camps are our reward for getting through the summer," he jokes.

During the winter, although Peter still conducts some nature walks, he switches to more indoor activities such as crafts. In addition, he plans for the spring and summer. He also does demonstrations for school classes with some of the live animals that live at Irvine.

## Lobsters and Moose

Peter grew up north of Boston. Family vacations near the ocean roused his interest in lobstering and fisheries. After high school, he majored in wildlife management at the University of Vermont. His courses prepared him to design and conduct scientific studies aimed at protecting wildlife. They haven't helped him teach people about nature, though. "Wildlife management is more statistical," he says.

After graduation, Peter took a summer job studying gypsy moths for the U.S. Forest Service. By fall, he was selling and delivering lobsters. Then a friend told him about volunteer jobs with the Alaska Department of Fish and Game. Although these jobs didn't pay, they offered room and board and priceless experience. Peter soon found himself tagging, or marking, Alaskan salmon

during their migration to the sea. After 11 months, he transferred to the wildlife division to conduct nutritional and behavioral studies of moose on the Kenai Peninsula. Five months later, he was back to salmon studies, this time to evaluate where fish ladders—which look like waterslides and help the salmon return to their spawning grounds—should be built. Peter worked in Alaska for another six months before returning to Massachusetts.

Next came a move to Maryland. Driving around his new neighborhood, Peter saw a sign for the Irvine Natural Science Center and soon became a volunteer. A month later, he was offered a job. "I was in the right place at

**Naturalists can help people become more comfortable with animals and other aspects of the natural world.**

the right time," he says. At first he worked in the center's bookstore and maintained the buildings and gardens. Teaching came later.

## Future of Outdoor Education

Outdoor educators, Peter believes, may have a tough time finding jobs in the future. He fears the grant money that private organizations and governments give to support nature programs will become increasingly scarce. Another change will be the use of technology, such as CD-ROM, to teach about animals and their habitats. However, only the largest and best-funded natural science centers can afford computers. "Computers in the exhibit room would be interesting," says Peter. "We'd be fairly high-tech if we had more money." New jobs will be created by the technology, he believes, including positions for software writers and computer graphic artists who are knowledgeable about outdoor education.

When asked about his own future, Peter is honest: "I absolutely don't know. I think about it all the time." The logical next step, he says, would be a job as an education director, perhaps with an environmental organization. But that would require a lot more administrative and computer work for him, something he's not sure he wants. "It's hard for me to organize," he says. "It's what I found frustrating about this job. I also like the opportunity to get outside and do bird-watching and hiking." For now, Peter plans to continue his work at Irvine, creating new programs as the center continues to grow.

# Outdoor Education

Outdoor educators work for natural science centers, zoos, wildlife preserves, and for national, state, and local parks. Environmental organizations, such as the National Wildlife Federation, also hire outdoor educators. Private organizations pay adventure-minded naturalists to lead expeditions into the wild, sometimes for a week or more. A bachelor's degree in biology, ecology, outdoor education, or wildlife management is typically required of most naturalists.

Some careers in outdoor education—such as raising money for new programs—may have few outdoor responsibilities. Park rangers and wildlife managers, for example, may do interpretive, or educational, programs for the public, but their main emphasis is on research or the preservation of parks and wildlife. Outfitters, who don't need degrees, are experienced at survival in the wilderness under difficult conditions. In all cases, a career in outdoor recreation requires love, knowledge, and respect for nature. Jobs can be scarce, low-paying, and may mean moving to another part of the country. Internships—listed in nature magazines—are great for getting experience.

**Park rangers teach tourists about the history and wildlife in national and state parks.**

Chris Trump

# Chapter Ten

# ACTIVITIES DIRECTOR

obody here knows my name," says Chris Trump. He's not kidding. As the activities director in a nursing home, he supervises 20 elderly residents—mostly women—who are in the last stages of Alzheimer's disease. "Their bodies are fine," he says. "It's their minds that have deteriorated." Alzheimer's disease destroys short-term memory, leaving people confused and unable to care for themselves. There is no cure or treatment. "I never thought I'd be doing this in a million years," Chris says. "I thought I'd play professional soccer."

Working with Alzheimer's patients is a job filled with joy, frustration, and sadness. "These people were productive in their lifetime," Chris says. "I try to give them the best quality of life for as long as I can." Then he sighs. "You see some people on the decline and in a constant state of anxiety. I come home physically and mentally exhausted."

## Structured Day

Chris works from 9:30 A.M. to 5:30 P.M., Monday through Friday, in the Alzheimer's unit of a Maryland nursing home. Mornings begin with a social hour of coffee and discussion. Chris reads aloud from newspaper articles, usually choosing opinion columns such as Dear Abby to spark conversation. "People are not as easily distracted in the morning," he says. Three nursing assistants make sure residents don't wander off.

At 11, Chris leads residents through a series of stretching exercises. More vigorous exercise—such as shooting baskets—comes next. "Everybody claps when someone makes a basket," he says. After lunch, Chris talks with each resident individually, then organizes a group discussion. That's followed by trivia games such as naming the presidents. By 2 P.M., residents are ready for snacks. Then comes another round of exercise, perhaps shuffleboard or balloon volleyball.

"I've found that with these people, I need a structured day," says Chris. "I keep the same time frame for each activity. And I keep each activity under 30 minutes." At 3 P.M. he offers arts and crafts, such as painting or sculpting with clay. At 3:45 P.M., there is a rest period before the afternoon movie—usually a musical, such as *The Sound of Music*. His work day is over at 5:30 P.M.

On Wednesdays, an activities assistant frees Chris to do administrative work. He arranges for musical entertainers, such as keyboard players or a barbershop quartet. He also prepares his monthly budget and orders sports equipment and snacks. Every three months, he writes an activities plan for each resident. He outlines his goals for that person and what approach caregivers should take. If, for example, someone has a hearing problem, he might suggest that everyone make a point of speaking loudly to that person.

## World Class Soccer

Chris grew up in Maryland, playing soccer from the time he was six. During high school, he was chosen for state and national teams. American University in Washington, D.C., gave him a soccer scholarship. He chose a business major but dropped out after one year. "I didn't think college was for me," he says. Taking a year off to travel and think, he supported himself through odd jobs such as waiting tables. He returned to school at

> ## I never thought I'd be doing this in a million years.

Montgomery College near his home, then transferred to Flagler College in Florida. By this time, playing soccer professionally had become less important to him. "When I took that year off, I found out that life is about more than soccer," he says.

At Flagler, Chris majored in recreation management, a program that gave him college credit for two internships. During the

first internship, at a YMCA, he worked 40 hours a week. "I coached, officiated at games, and supervised the aquatics program," he says. "I did a little bit of everything." He also began a "Time-Out" program to help kids with their homework. His second internship was at a facility for mentally handicapped people. "I ran activities," he says. "I would have bingo, weight lifting, and basketball." Summers during college he worked as a counselor at American and Georgetown Universities' soccer camps. After graduation, Chris taught physical education as a substitute teacher for a year before taking his current job.

## Compassion and Humor

If there's anything that has surprised Chris about working in a nursing home, it's his own kindness toward the elderly residents. "I didn't know I was such a compassionate person," he says. He spends time with them, making jokes and comforting conversation. "I work through humor. The greatest medicine is laughter all day. I have to be an entertainer." Although it's fulfilling for Chris to get a smile or a laugh from a resident, he also gets frustrated. "I hate losing people who are almost good friends to me," he says. "It's a very hands-on job. I do a lot of physical contact—hugs and pats on the back. I can't not become attached."

Chris also faces questions from the families of residents. "Families come to me to ask how their mother is doing," he says. He knows how hard it is for them to accept that their loved one with Alzheimer's disease is never going to recover.

## A Career for the Future

Chris doesn't plan to work with Alzheimer's patients forever. "It's too taxing mentally," he says. "I like being around sports. I'd love to be coaching kids 10 to 15 years old. I want to teach people who take soccer seriously." He knows it won't be easy to get a full-time job, since many government recreation centers have cut back their programs.

Chris expects the number of jobs working with the elderly to increase as more people grow older and need care. "I think it's a good idea to get started early," he says. Often nursing homes welcome teenage volunteers to help residents with arts and crafts or bring their pets to visit. Teens can also work as nursing aides. "You need to see the environment," he says, "to see people who are old, to see if you can take it."

**Physical activity helps people stay healthy. Older people who stay active are less likely to fall and break bones.**

**Di Goodman**

# Chapter Eleven

# SAILING INSTRUCTOR

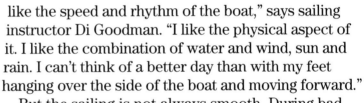

"I like the speed and rhythm of the boat," says sailing instructor Di Goodman. "I like the physical aspect of it. I like the combination of water and wind, sun and rain. I can't think of a better day than with my feet hanging over the side of the boat and moving forward."

But the sailing is not always smooth. During bad weather, Di must show confidence and inspire trust. Strong communication skills are vital, too. "You have to be in charge," she says. "Many people are apprehensive. You have to be calm. There is one captain on every boat. You have to be it." She also needs to be in good physical condition. "In a storm," she says, "I rely on my body to manage the boat."

## The Sailing Season

Thousands of people from all over the country come to the Annapolis Sailing School where Di teaches. The sailing season lasts from March through October. She often teaches seven days a week. "It's the only time you have to make money," she says. "You can't work in the winter."

A typical weekend sailing workshop begins at 8 A.M. on Saturday. Di and the other instructors pilot the 24-foot teaching boats to the dock, swab off the algae and mud, and see that the safety equipment is on board. Each sailboat holds four students and one instructor. At nine o'clock, students attend the first of four lectures. Using a chalkboard, videotapes, and a sailboat model, Di goes over the basics of sailing, explaining how the wind moves the boat and the use of the safety equipment.

At 10 A.M., the students get their first taste of actual sailing. Di shows them how to put the sails on and how to steer. At noon, they return to the dock for lunch. By one o'clock, everybody is back in the classroom. Di answers questions about the morning sail, then talks about the "rules of the road." At two o'clock, students are on the water again, learning about the points of sailing, or the relative angles of the boat to the wind. At four, they dock the boats, then take down and fold the sails. The instructors scrub down the boats and link them in a chain out on the

# " Anyone who teaches sailing knows that this is someone's vacation. "

water to protect them from banging against the dock.

The whole process starts over the next morning. "It can be a grind," Di says. "You don't always feel like teaching beginners. But anyone who teaches sailing knows that this is someone's vacation. It's not okay to be curt, or short-tempered, or tired."

**Annapolis Sailing School**

Di didn't grow up sailing. She took her first course at the Annapolis Sailing School when she was 16. "I really liked the whole experience. I became a good racer," she says. The summer after high school graduation, she became a sailing instructor. That was 15 years ago. She has

Di Goodman

taught every summer since, including during her college years at Johns Hopkins University where she studied writing.

After college graduation, Di worked for a few months selling yachts, then became a sales representative for an educational publisher. She moved to upstate New York, and later to New Jersey. Living far away meant driving long hours back to Annapolis each summer weekend to teach. After five years of selling and marketing textbooks to schools and colleges, she decided the work was not right for her.

# Certification

To teach sailing, you must be certified by the U.S. Sailing Association, the governing body for the sport. There are two levels: dinghy and keelboat. Summer camp counselors are usually dinghy certified to teach on small boats. Di is keelboat certified and qualified to teach and captain boats up to 40 feet long. "A 40-foot boat," she says, "is a major piece of equipment." Both certifications require instructors to pass written and practical tests of their fundamental sailing skills, knowledge of first aid, and mastery of classroom teaching.

Di is now studying for her U.S. Coast Guard captain's license, which will allow her to pilot boats up to 200 feet long. Boats this size include tankers and excursion boats, such as the ones that take tourists out for day trips in the Chesapeake

Bay. Only sailors with 365 eight-hour days on the water qualify to take the Coast Guard's difficult written test. In addition, Di is certified for CPR and first aid by the American Red Cross.

**The bigger the boat, the more training its captain needs.**

# First-Aid Training

P.E. teachers, camp counselors, and recreation leaders often need to complete first-aid and water safety instruction. Local branches of the American Red Cross offer a variety of classes and certifications. Training is often held at community colleges. Courses vary in length, from 6 to 40 hours. Most include video instruction and hands-on practice, followed by written and practical tests. Basic aid training—an American Red Cross certificate program for students aged 8 to 13—focuses on the prevention of injuries and ways to handle emergencies.

Di's next job was writing *The Student Environmental Action Guide* with another author. She enjoyed the research and writing, and the eight-month project enabled her to move back to Annapolis. Then she wrote a book, *Learning to Sail*, with Ian Brodie. The following fall, Di began law school at the University of Baltimore.

Di isn't sure about her future. "I want to do something with writing and the law," she says. "Sailing is seasonal. It's helpful to have other sources of income."

## Sailing's Future

Because sailing is an expensive sport, its popularity is related to how much money people can spend on recreation. "Summer camps will always provide opportunities for people to learn to sail," Di says. The 1990s have brought more interest in family sailing, with kids learning alongside their parents. Di sometimes takes out families for a week of sailing around the Chesapeake Bay.

The technology of sailing is also changing. At the Annapolis Sailing School, she says, "We still do all our navigation with pen,

pencil, dividers, and charts." As radar and electrical navigation systems become more advanced, sailors will need to know how to use on-board computers.

What will remain the same is what it takes to teach sailing: resourcefulness, physical fitness, strong fundamental skills, and a first-rate ability to communicate. Although Di warns that teaching sailing is usually not a full-time career, she understands its attraction. "What's great about sailing is being outdoors, being with people and teaching. It gets under your skin."

Di advises potential sailors to "read a lot about sailing." Although she took the course she now teaches, many people learn through experience. "Summer camp is a good way to start," she says. "You have to learn the fundamentals."

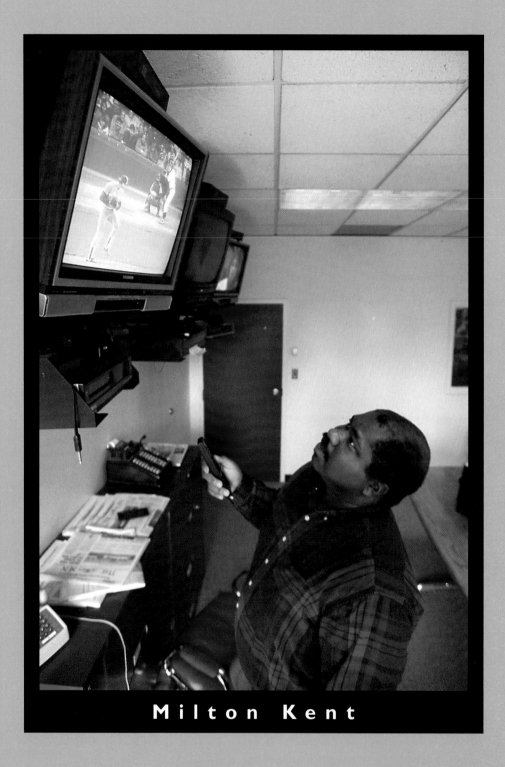

Milton Kent

# Chapter Twelve

# SPORTSWRITER

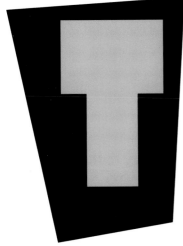

"Television dictates when games are played, how they are played, and where they are played," says sports columnist Milton Kent. "I take satisfaction in getting readers to understand what they watch." Milton writes "On the Air," a column about television sports coverage. The column appears five days a week in the *Baltimore Sun*. He also writes about women's college basketball.

Milton never played sports. "But I've always loved sports and watching sports events," he says. He also always loved words. "As a kid, writing was something I enjoyed doing. This is a good field for me."

## Distractions and Interruptions

Milton works Sunday through Thursday. Since television and radio networks supply him with a daily flood of press releases and announcements, he checks his mail and faxes when he arrives at the office around 10 A.M. Then his phone begins to ring. Publicists for the networks call him constantly with information. Even his readers call. The interruptions can drive him crazy when he's busy. "Readers call to ask what game is on," he says with exasperation.

The *Sun's* crowded, buzzing newsroom is filled with the sound of ringing phones and conversations between staffers under deadline pressure. Milton has learned to concentrate despite the noise. "I drift through the day," he says. "Every day is different." When he is writing, he often dons earphones and tunes to a jazz station to block out the noise. "Writing is very hard even if I'm not distracted," he says.

At least once a week, Milton takes part in a telephone press conference. For example, NBC held a conference to publicize its coverage of the NBA All-Star Game. Three NBC announcers answered questions about players and the game submitted by sports columnists from newspapers across the country. "You listen to someone on the other end ask questions," he says, "and try to think of something else if someone asks your question." He scribbles notes in longhand.

The networks also send information to reporters. Milton points to a fat binder that ABC Sports prepared about its Super Bowl coverage. And his desk is littered with videos, for example, a tape from CBS to promote a program about the Olympics. He estimates that he spends about 20 hours a week watching sports on television.

Throughout the day, Milton reads faxes, talks with fellow reporters, talks on the phone, and thinks about his column. He may use his laptop computer to check out the on-line sports services or do some research. "Some days you know what you're going to

write," he says, referring to the big sports stories that are in the news. Since most sporting events take place on weekends, Mondays and Fridays are the easiest. Other days, he may choose a single topic or include random items about televised sports. "I don't panic any more about it," he says.

Around four in the afternoon, Milton begins to write. His column runs 12 to 20 column inches—approximately 700 words. It's longer during football season. He writes for about an hour to an hour and a half. On Sundays he writes at home. His column then goes to a copy editor, who corrects any spelling or grammar mistakes and makes sure

# Writing is very hard even if I'm not distracted.

the column reads well.

Since the *Sun* recently upgraded its computer system, Milton hopes he will soon be able to work at home all the time, returning to the office only to fill out his expense accounts and attend meetings. His workday ends around 7 P.M.

**The Newspaper**

Milton has spent his entire career with the *Baltimore Sun*. The paper awarded him a scholarship—which included four paid

# Sports Careers in Publishing

Sportswriting is not limited to newspapers. Many magazines, from *Sports Illustrated* to *Tennis* and *Cycle,* also employ sportswriters. Writers can be on staff or freelance. The editors who choose and edit stories, however, almost always work full time. Editing—like writing—is a job that requires attention to detail, an ability to work under pressure, a good vocabulary, computer skills, and some knowledge of sports.

Many editors have degrees in English or journalism. Pay varies depending on the size of the circulation of the newspaper or magazine. Competition for full-time jobs is intense.

Another related career is sports photography. Magazines and newspapers use both staff and freelance photographers. Experience and a first-rate portfolio are more important than a college degree. Sports photographers work long hours under fast-moving, sometimes difficult conditions.

summer internships—to study journalism at
the University of Maryland. "Internships are
key," he says. "It's the only way to have
someone in the business find out what you
can do." His four summers added up to an on-
the-job training program.

His first summer at the *Sun,* Milton
answered phones and sorted mail. He
graduated to writing stories about parades or
college events. By the third summer, he was
writing news stories for the evening paper.
"The staff treated me like a functioning

Milton Kent

Radio and television sportscasters who describe the action, as it happens, during a sporting event are doing the *play-by-play.* A second sportscaster may provide the *color commentary:* other, related information about the players or the game.

adult," he says. "I needed help here and there, but mostly they left me alone."

During the school year, Milton worked Saturdays at the *Sun.* He also volunteered as a disc jockey at the college radio station and did color commentary for basketball games. As another announcer called the play-by-play, Milton gave background information about the players and games. After being elected sports director of the station, Milton called the play-by-play for basketball games during his junior and senior years.

Milton's first full-time job at the *Sun* took him to a satellite office in a nearby county. He covered government, politics, police activities, and schools. Two and a half years later, he was assigned to the metro section. "I came in at 2 P.M. and covered anything that happened until 10 P.M.," he says. When the features department was short a reporter, he became the rock music critic for a year.

Transferred to sports, Milton covered men's and women's college basketball for three years, then landed a glamor job as the backup reporter for the Baltimore Orioles. "The full-time beat reporter would cover the main game story," he says. Milton wrote the sidebars—stories about players having hot and cold streaks or a particularly noteworthy game. He had to go to the ballpark to do interviews. Because of the deadline pressure and intense reader interest in the Orioles, he says, "It was decidedly a pressure-filled job."

Milton doesn't know how long he'll write "On the Air." "My hope would be to do a more general-interest column someday," he says. He is also planning a book about college basketball.

**Technology**

Milton predicts that print journalism will continue to be changed by technology, with computers and television replacing newspapers. Readers will demand sports stories, not the next day but immediately following a game. "We'll be working even faster than we do now," he says. Sportswriters, he believes, will write about only one sport, rather than a variety.

Milton's advice—besides being an intern—is to take every opportunity to write and be published. School newspapers or magazines offer opportunities to do reporting on local sports events. *Sports Illustrated for Kids* publishes letters from readers. Curiosity is all-important, too, Milton says. "And you have to have a strong spirit because this is a business that can get you down," he says. "You have to work under pressure." He views an interest in sports as an advantage but not the most important thing. "The challenge of a writer is to tell the story in an entertaining way and take people a step beyond what they've seen on television," he says.

# To Continue Exploring...

Acupuncture Research Institute
313 W. Andrix Street
Monterey Park, CA 91754

Aerobics & Fitness Association of America
15250 Ventura Boulevard
Suite 200
Sherman Oaks, CA 91403

American Camping Association
5000 State Rd #67 North
Martinsville, IN 46151

American Council on Exercise
5820 Oberlin Drive
Suite 102
San Diego, CA 92121

American Red Cross
8111 Gatehouse Road
5th Floor
Falls Church, VA 22042

American Sportscasters Association
5 Beekman Street
Suite 814
New York, NY 10038

National Association for Sport and Physical
   Education
1900 Association Drive
Reston, VA 22091

National Association of Activity Professionals
1225 I Street, NW
Suite 300
Washington, DC 20005

National Athletic Trainers' Association
2952 Stemmons Freeway
Suite 200
Dallas, TX 75247

National Collegiate Athletic Association
6201 College Boulevard
Overland Park, KS 66211

National Federation Interscholastic Coaches'
   Association
11724 N.W. Plaza Circle
Kansas City, MO 64195

National High School Athletic Coaches'
   Association
Box 941329
Maitland, FL 32794

National Recreation and Parks Association
2775 S. Quincy Street
Suite 300
Arlington, VA 22206

National Sportscasters and Sportswriters
   Association
Box 559
Salisbury, NC 28144

National Youth Sports Association
2611 Old Okeechobee Road
W. Palm Beach, FL 33409

Outdoor Educators Association
143 Foxhill Road
Denville, NJ 07834

Special Olympics International
1350 New York Avenue, NW
Washington, DC 20005

U.S. Sailing Association
P.O. Box 209
Newport, RI 02840

U.S. Tennis Association
70 West Red Oak Lane
White Plains, NY 10604

# INDEX

personal health trainers, 24
photographers, 34, 104, 105
physical education (P.E.)
teachers, 19, 40, 54, 58,
64, 70, 73, 74, 88;
education needed for, 39,
72, 96
physical therapists, 42, 70
physical therapy
technicians, 42
play-by-play announcers,
35, 106
producers, 29, 30, 32, 33, 34
professional sports
careers, 48. *See also*
shortstops

recreation assistants, 64,
73
recreation leaders, 64, 96
recruiters, 14, 15
reporters, 32, 34, 106. *See
also* sportscasters,
television; sportswriters

sailing instructors:
certification needed for,
95; getting started in
career, 93–94, 98;
personality of, 93;
responsibilities of,
91–93, 97; skills of, 91,
98; work hours of, 91–92
scholarships, 16, 47, 87, 103
school program directors:
competition for jobs of,
58; education needed for,
55; getting started in
career, 57, 58; other jobs
relating to, 59;
responsibilities of, 53,
54–55, 58; skills of, 58;
work hours of, 54
scouts, 16, 49
self-employment, 24. *See
also* freelance work
shortstops: competition for
jobs of, 45; education
needed for, 47, 51; getting
started in career, 49–50,
51; personality of, 46–47;

responsibilities of, 46;
salaries of, 45–46, 48;
work hours of, 46
soccer, 18, 61, 62, 63–64,
85, 87, 88
softball, 39, 64, 70. *See
also* baseball
software writers, 82
Special Olympics, 18,
69–70, 73–75
Special Olympics
administrators:
education needed for,
71, 73, 74; getting
started in career,
73–74, 75; other jobs
relating to, 72;
personality of, 75;
responsibilities of,
69–71; work hours of,
70
sportscasters, television:
competition for jobs of,
33; education needed
for, 31, 32–33; getting
started in career, 31–32,
35; other jobs relating
to, 34; responsibilities
of, 29–31, 32, 33;
salaries of, 34; skills of,
33; work hours of, 30,
31
sports coordinators, 63
sports facility managers:
education needed for,
63–64, 66–67; getting
started in career, 64, 67;
other jobs relating to,
65; responsibilities of,
61–63, 64; skills of, 62,
64, 66; work hours of,
62
sports management field,
59
sports medicine. *See*
athletic trainers
sports segment
producers, 34
sportswriters: getting
started in career,
105–106, 107; other

jobs relating to, 104;
personality of, 107;
responsibilities of,
101–103, 105–106;
training needed for, 103,
105; work hours of, 101,
103
student trainers, 39, 40
swimming, 38

technology, 82, 97–98, 107.
*See also* computers
tennis, 39, 48, 53–55,
57–58

umpires, 64, 65
U.S. Sailing Association,
56, 95
U.S. Tennis Association
(USTA), 53–55, 58;
Education Committee, 57

volleyball, 18, 50, 69–70
volunteer work, 14, 17, 31,
57, 58, 79, 80–81, 106;
during high school, 18,
31, 43, 67, 75, 89. *See also*
internships; on-the-job
training

weekend sportscasters, 32,
34
wildlife managers, 80, 83
writers, 62, 97. *See also*
sportswriter

## ABOUT THE AUTHOR

Barbara Lee is the author of *Death in Still Waters: A Chesapeake Bay Mystery*, which won St. Martin's Press' 1994 Best First Malice Domestic Mystery Novel Contest. A New Yorker, she now lives in Maryland.

### ACKNOWLEDGMENTS

The photographs in this book are reproduced with the permission of: pp. 2, 33, 41, 97, Rob Tringali Jr./SportsChrome East/West; p. 6, SportsChrome East/West; pp. 10, 12, 15, 19, 28, 30, 31, 32, 36, 39, 43, 44, 47, 52, 55, 57, 60, 63, 66, 68, 70, 71, 76, 78, 79, 81, 84, 87, 89, 90, 92, 93, 94, 98, 100, 103, Andy King; pp. 14, 17, 18, Courtesy of the Amateur Athletic Union; p. 16, Northwest Racquet, Swim & Health Clubs, Minneapolis, Minnesota; pp. 20, 22, 23, 26, Mario Villafuerte; pp. 24, 95, Carnival Cruise Lines; p. 34, Mike Corrado/SportsChrome East/West; p. 35, Nancy Smedstad/IPS, Courtesy of Fox 29; pp. 40, 83, 96, 99, Billy Barnes; pp. 48, 49, 50, 65, 104, 109, 110, Shmuel Thaler; p. 56, Courtesy of Camp Icaghowan; p. 59, Bruce Bennett Studios; p. 72, Betts Anderson, Unicorn Stock Photos; pp. 73, 75, © Special Olympics International; p. 105, Nancy Smedstad/IPS, Courtesy of the St. Paul Pioneer Press; p. 107, Nancy Smedstad/IPS.